The Christ
Conscious Mind

Francis Egbokhare

The Christ Conscious Mind

Francis Egbokhare

Francis Egbokhare

National Library of Nigeria Cataloguing-in-Publication
Data

Contents

FOREWORD

From time to time we take a break from our busy world to reflect, meditate and pray. Sometimes, we have the good sense to put down impressions that seem compelling. When we get back to our notes, we may have an urge to share our thoughts and opinions.

This collection gives my perspective on a number of issues bordering on my Christian life and responsibility. There is a bit more for the general reader who is not impressed by religion. I have written primarily for those who would like to be known as Christians.

The first three chapters deal with Christian lifestyle, responsibility and righteousness. Chapter four to nine take on different topics form faith and works, attitude, dignity of labour and my thoughts on life held together by the foundations of faith.

You may not agree with all that is set out in this modest work, but I hope it gets you thinking. This was never meant to be more than just a bedside nugget for those who truly and honestly desire personal change. I hope you find something positive to reflect on and talk about as you read on.

"YE ARE THE LIGHT OF THE WORLD; A CITY THAT IS SET ON A HILL CANNOT BE HID. NEITHER DO MEN LIGHT A CANDLE AND PUT IT UNDER A BUSHEL, BUT ON A CANDLE STICK; AND IT GIVETH LIGHT UNTO ALL THAT ARE IN THE OUSE. LET YOUR LIGHT SO SHINE BEFORE MEN, THAT THEY MAY SEE YOUR GOOD WORKS AND GLORIFY YOUR FATHER IN HEAVEN."

Matthew 5: 13-16

CHAPTER 1
The Christian Lifestyle

"Ye are the salt of the earth; but if the salt have lost his saviour, wherewith shall it be salted? It is henceforth good for nothing, but to be cast out, and to be trodden under foot of men."

". . .if therefore the light that is in you be darkness, how great is that darkness!" (Matt. 6: 23)

What was Christ really saying to His disciples thousands of years ago? He was frustrated at the worldliness of the disciples; perhaps He had difficulties in telling them apart from others; perhaps He was getting frustrated that His message was not getting through. His disciples were living like mere men, sinning, revealing, engaging in idolatry, etc. Christ was saying, don't you know who you are? Don't you know your heritage?

Three symbols are used in the passage in Matt. 5: 13-16. These are (a) light, (b) salt, (c) a city (on a hill). They form the basis of the metaphors that encapsulate the Christian lifestyle. Light guides and pertains to leadership (Matt. 15: 14: the blind cannot lead the blind). Salt seasons and pertains to character, that is, being a role model. Salt refers not to the situation in the world where role modelling is defined by media presence or visibility, it is founded on humility. A city or house is a dwelling place, a refuge. This pertains to love, compassion, and service (Isaiah 61: 1-3). Christian love is sacrificial not sensual. The symbols of light, salt and house capture the form, content and purpose of our life as Christians. The purpose of our life is to glorify God, otherwise it lacks divine value.

Service is emphasized by the fact that we are not just a city but one on a hill, not hidden but exposed; visible. We are not just under a bushel but on a table to serve others. Being light, salt or a city describes inherent qualities which may be useless if they are hidden. We must put our qualities to use for men. Perhaps the disciples were busy trying to identify with every fashionable trend. They were busy throwing big parties, taking chieftaincy titles. Perhaps it was the kind of music they were making, perhaps one could not tell them apart by their manner of speech; their style of living may not have set them apart. Perhaps Christ found out they still had very keen eyes on the world. He could see that every worldly practice was ingenuously adapted to the church setting; the worship of men, the pursuit of material things, hatred, malice, envying, strife and lust. Let your light so shine that men may see it and glorify your father in heaven. The primary purpose of the Christian life is to give glory to God.

Foundations of the Christian Lifestyle

Lifestyle refers to a person's or group's characteristic manner of living; one's style of life. Culture, status, religion, profession and psychological make-up, among others, determine a person's lifestyle. It is a function of the way we are brought up, or experience, expectations, and so on. The Christian lifestyle is determined by the kind of relationship which we have with Christ; our submission to His will, immersion in His word, conformity to His image and detachment from world patterns. It is a function of who reigns in our life and in which kingdom we thrive (Luke 6: 47; John 15: 4-5).

The Christian lifestyle is full of paradoxes. A paradox is a statement that may be true but seems to say the opposite. The Christian lives physically in the world but spiritually she/he is not of the world. Her / His standards are not of the world but s/he applies them to world situations. S/he is under physical rule of men but God reigns in her/ his life. She/he works in the world economy but is governed by heavenly ethics. She/he earns earthly wages but makes investments in heavenly treasures.

She/he is born of a woman but not of flesh. She/he is dead but lives through Christ. She/he strives on earth but her/ his inheritance is in heaven. She/he works under men but has God as her/ his master. She/he dwells in earthly kingdom, but her/his citizenship is of heaven.

The bible is very clear that there are two lifestyles. There is a worldly one and heavenly one and both patterns are opposed. Paul, writing to the Romans says, "I beseech you therefore, brethren, by the mercies of God, that ye present your bodies a living sacrifice, holy, acceptable unto God, which is your reasonable service. And be not conformed to this world . . . (Rom 12: 1-2). "Love not the world, neither the things that are in the world. If any man loves the world, the love of the father is not in him" (1 John 2: 15-16). Following a similar pattern, James (4:4) states that "friendship with the world is enmity with God". If these scriptures have not defined clearly the existence of the two paradigms, Matt (6: 24) does it clearly by showing that both of them are irreconcilable. "NO man can serve two masters; for either he will hate one and love the other or else he will hold to the one and despise the other. Ye cannot serve God and Mammon".

How then should a Christian live in practical terms? Conversely, how should a Christian not live? Titus 2: 12 states ". . . that denying ungodliness and worldly lust, we should live soberly, righteously and godly, in this present world. Our lifestyle should be one that emphasises humility, meekness, temperance, gentleness, love, joy and peace (Gal 5: 22-23). Open display of wealth, ostentatious and vain living; showmanship and so called power dressing do not agree with the principle of moderation. "Let your moderation be known unto all men. The Lord is at hand" (Phil. 4:5). Heb. 13: 5 admonishes us to ". . . be content with such things as ye have". This is quite the contrary to a lifestyle driven by greed and ambition. Parents abandon children to stay abroad for years to make money. Many pastors forge documents to travel abroad for ministration. Many Christians marry official wives in foreign countries to obtain residence permit. Many more things there are which we do that appear reasonable but are clearly driven by worldliness. Consider how we often get false bank statements so that we can obtain visas to travel to other countries. Are churches now not preaching materialism? Is Christianity not now reduced to an ideology? Is spirituality not equated with excitement? Many have substituted the message of salvation with psychology. Several preachers are simply motivational speakers and among our leaders are those who are better regarded as mystics. Many Christians belong to societies in the world or village unions with principles and practices that are anti-Christ and unprogressive.

You may ask what is wrong with village unions. I would say that Christians should not be found wherever people seek to gain advantage over others, wherever people perpetrate tribalism, wherever favouritism and unjust practices are encouraged. Envying, ambition, emulations, seditions, etc., are some patterns of a worldly life. (Gal. 5: 19-26). The church has now imbibed a lot of these patterns in prayers and worldly music. We tend to import all worldly practices in our worship and sanctify them in Jesus' name. What of burial practices, the waste, the ritual, the deception, the display of wealth in the face of poverty and hunger within the congregation? What about weddings – the multiple weddings all in the name of introduction, engagement, court and church ceremonies. These are done in conformity to culture, status and prevailing fashion. Christians are supposed to bring about change; not to perpetuate unprogressive ideas. Non-conformity with worldly patterns, separation from worldly patterns,, separation from worldly practices, non-entanglement with prevailing practices are hallmarks of a Christian lifestyle (Rom. 12:2; Gal. 5: 1-2; Tim. 2:4)

A Christian life must be founded on humility, the form of which is meekness and the expression of which is submission. We submit first of all to God and to authorities. When humility is lacking in a soul, our good works become sterile activism, radicalism becomes mere rascality, courage is nothing but foolhardiness, service is masked in ambition, charity becomes nothing more than showmanship; we become the centre of the world, the standard and measure by which the world must be judged and evaluated.

"By humility, we win God's heart, and by gentleness we attract

and win over the hearts of our brothers".

(Salvatores Canals).

Without meekness, we are noisy, bossy, and authoritarian. Meekness imbues us with friendliness, good manners and respect for others.

Sacrifice is the salt of the Christian life. Without sacrifice, there can be no service. Service rendered without sacrifice is mere ambition. A Christian has to die metaphorically (Matt. 10: 37-39; John 15: 13; Rom. 8:13; Gal. 2:20). A Christian has to live as if she/he were not important. The Christian must focus on the common good. It is not possible to work as part of a body, in a team, without the loss of self, the surrender of ego. Without self-denial, we are only capable of individuality, not community. There is a heavy cost associated with the Christian lifestyle. It may lead to the loss of status, of position, loss of dignity and suffering.

Luke 9: 62 states that no one who puts his hands on the plough and looks back is fit for the kingdom of God. The service a Christian offers must be driven by focus, single-minded devotion, commitment and discipline. Our work must be done as if our very life depends on it. We must serve other people with loyalty and dedication notwithstanding their relationship with us, or their attitude towards us. We must do other people's jobs as if it were our own. We need to put other people's work on our heads not on our shoulders. We are called to be *Afamako*. The king's job must become our responsibility. Integrity and holiness must characterise our emblem and identity. However, today we know that these qualities are very rare amongst us. The better expression is 'eye service'. We need to ask ourselves basic questions in all honesty: Do we use official time for private business, for example? If we only work when the boss is around, we are heading for hell. The reason is, no one who has his or her hand on the plough and looks back is fit for the kingdom of God.

Do we stand out as Christians?

Do we stand out as Christians or are we being swallowed up by the crowd? The principle of separation, the symbols of light, salt and the city on a hill; the call to be disciples are all united in the fact that Christians are called to a life of excellence, a distinctive and remarkable life; a distinguished one. The world is a dark place and there is enough darkness already. We are all supposed to be light sparks wherever we are and together we can become a mighty conflagration, a great fire. "If the light in us be darkness, how great is that darkness indeed?" Do not be deceived by your many prayers or your talents which you have come to promote above the fruits of true Christian essence. We are called to make a difference. Wherever we find darkness, we need to give light. In places where pride pervades we need to show humility; where men have become vain, sobriety becomes our only option. In the face of a culture of greed and materialism, our cross is to accept contentment and live soberly. Where there is strife and hatred we need to teach love; and where men form cleavages we should be the bridge that unites. We are so far tossed and thrown up and down in the sea of vanity. Our preachers live and show off as kings in the face of poverty. They preach greed and materialism and mislead people to believe that this is prosperity. The bible has become a talisman; the name of Jesus is a magic wand. When men are selfish, we think they are meek; when they are unruly, we identify them as radical. This is because we are swallowed up in darkness.

Let us look at some of the things we do and reflect on them:

a. Over 70% of civil servants arrive late to work and several close early. Most people do not genuinely earn their wages.
b. Obtaining sick leave falsely, false age declaration, false tax declaration, etc.
c. Ethnic chauvinism: how many of us have close friends from other ethnic groups? How many will live under the authority of people from other ethnic groups?

d. Lobbying and influence peddling: do you lobby for positions? Do you go to seek the assistance of principalities and powers for appointments?

e. Bribery and corruption: in government offices, there are elaborate bribery and corruption schemes. Pastors, elders, evangelists, etc., share in the loot. Some are the direct receivers yet they wear collars. What a mockery! Where are the Christians in the Police force?

f. Examination fraud: how many of us parents send out children to coaching centres where we know that there is organized fraud? We send them there for that very reason! Do Christian invigilators not participate in examination fraud?

g. Double standard is not a virtue: we bend the rules for those we like and become rigid when it comes to others. Favouritism is a sin. University admission processes is ridden with this vice.

h. Giving false recommendations: we lie about a person and recommend him for a position. We call a dead devil a saint at burials; we tell lies about thieves to be in their good books. We honour evil people with titles and recommend evil as honourable.

i.   Littering of streets, reckless driving, jumping of queues, etc.

j.   Business practices; using false measures, manipulating customers, hoarding, inducements, building percentages into contracts, demanding gifts, etc.

k.   Various smuggling practices, obtaining fake customs papers, sale and purchase of driving licence and so on.

We cannot run through all the vices. However, it suffices to state that they are works of the flesh. A lifestyle is conditioned by character and convictions. Nigerian Christians know too much already about the bible – 'RELIGIOUS CONSPIRATION'. There is however a gap. Our problems seem to be how to translate visions to development, words to actions, actions to habits and knowledge to behaviour. We need to move from being opportunistic to being creative; from being instinctive to being reflective; from the force of nature to nurture; from being spontaneous to being strategic, from reacting to pro-acting. All these are a matter of lifestyle and Christians are in a unique position to make things happen positively in Nigeria. Christians must wake up from the kind of sterile positivism that has led to hypocrisy. We need to move

Francis Egbokhare

from preaching Christ to living Christ, from confessions to demonstrations and from faith to action. We need to remove the bushel from over the light, we need to extract the log from our eyes; we need to apply the salt to the soup. All these point to individual and corporate demonstration of commitment to faith. Preaching and talking about development will not bring about development. A change of perception needs to be followed by change of behaviour. What we needd today for development are commitment, focus and equity to foster a sense of community. To stimulate productivity, we need diligence and contentment.

The Christian lifestyle enables society to grow into communities; communities into nations. Individualism must give way to community; selfish interest must yield to common good. Sharing must be replaced by giving. Profit motive must give way to an attitude of service.

"TO SEE THE WEAKNESS AND WRONG IN OTHERS AND AT THE SAME TIME REFRAIN FROM JUDGING THEM . . . IS INDEED A NARROW WAY. THE WAY IS UNUTTERABLY HARD, AND AT EVERY MOMENT WE ARE IN DANGER OF STRAYING FROM IT".

Dietrich Boenhoffer

CHAPTER 2
Christian Responsibility: The Narrow and Rough Way

"Enter ye at the straight gate: for wide is the gate, and broad is the way, that leadeth to destruction, and many there be which go in there at: because straight is the gate, and narrow is the way, which leadeth unto life, and few there be that find it" (Matt. 7: 13-14) (NKJV). Dietrich Boenhoffer expands the above when he states that:

> The path of discipleship is narrow, and it is fatally easy to miss one's way and stray from the path, even after years of discipleship . . . On either side of the narrow path deep chasms yawn. To be called to a life of extraordinary quality, to live up to it, and yet to be unconscious of it is indeed a narrow way . . . to love our enemies with the infinite love of Jesus Christ . . . to face our enemies unarmed and defenceless, preferring to incur injustice rather than to

do wrong ourselves, is indeed a narrow way. To see the weakness and wrong in others and at the same time refrain from judging them . . . is indeed a narrow way. The way is unutterably hard, hard and at every moment we are in danger of straying from it (1937: 170).

The narrow way is not just a way of historical times it applies even to us today to be in an examination where everyone is cheating and to prefer to fail; to be in a political dispensation where people rig elections and prefer to lose or even not participate than to be declared a winner in a compromised election is indeed a narrow way. To lose power and prestige; to refuse to follow the bandwagon; to be poor, forsaken and irrelevant on account of what you believe; to stand up against falsehood, corruption, social vices and reject peer pressure than to be involved in drugs is indeed a narrow way. The narrow way is the way of personal sacrifice, the way of Christian responsibility.

We celebrated our 50th independence anniversary. As usual it has been a time of complaints and name calling. A time when many expresses their disappointment at the entity called Nigeria. It was a time when we isolated certain individuals whom we labelled leaders. I have often asked myself about my share of the blame in the sordid state of Nigeria. As I try to do a personal evaluation of my commitment, as I analyse the depth of my service, as I ruminate over the quality of my citizenship, as I ask what Christ would do at a time like this, I am unable to absolve myself of blame and I cannot honestly see the devil in others but in myself. A time will come when each of us must ask ourselves what our role has been in the fate of Nigeria. How much of our negligence accounts for the high rate of maternal deaths? How much of corruption is responsible for the high mortality rate? How have we contributed to the decay in infrastructure, low productivity and failure of our educational system? We are the ones who miss our periods in schools. We are the ones who report to work late. We cheat on our tax forms, we cheat on age, we sell drivers' licences without testing those who we give them to; yet we blame the devil for the road carnages. We celebrate with relatives who defraud the people and give them titles for a piece of the action; yet, we mourn over the poverty of the majority. When we have the upper hand, it is no use to talk of justice, but when we lose the advantage, we call for the world to end. He, who is guilty, let him or her cast the first stone.

Change must begin with a revolution of methods and a new definition of Christian discipleship. We have to imbibe Christianity and its religious activities as a lifestyle beyond its memory work. At the point at which we begin to take personal responsibility for the problems in our society, we have a chance of becoming relevant in the process of finding solutions to the issues that plague our generation. As Christians, we need to move away from the practices of the world and always ask ourselves what Christ would have us do. If Christ was a teacher, how would He teach? If He were a doctor, how would He treat His patients? If He were a banker, what would be His approach to banking? Would He be more interested in the mad competition for profits notwithstanding mass poverty? How would Christ drive His car? What will be His attitude to politics? We can plead all kinds of limitations and helplessness. We may say that we cannot act alone, but at least we can start alone, we can try. We may not be able to change the world, but we can change ourselves. The expectation of God has never been that we as individuals change the world but that we should be such good examples that men would give glory to God (Matt. 5: 14-16).

Responsible Christianity will start at the point when a Christian realises that his work matters to God, and that, religious activities without social responsibilities is mere activism. True Christian service can be measured only by its sacrifice. Sacrifice means putting others before self, embracing the common good and following Christ doggedly. We are the images of Christ in an uncreative world; salt to a bland and tasteless generation; we are sight to a people living in the region of darkness. There are great opportunities for Christians to shine in our country, yet we have chosen to follow the path of compromise. In great darkness, a flicker of light is a great hope. Imagine the great relief if some young Christians use an opportunity to clean their street weekly; imagine if some Christians volunteer to provide free services to a poor school in their neighbourhood; imagine if a bank lowers its interest rate to such levels as to permit the poor to borrow; imagine a doctor who will never go on strike so he can be of use to the sick; imagine if your church runs a school that the children of the poor can attend. We can go on and on but the point is that unless our righteousness surpasses that of the Pharisees, we shall likewise perish. When will it ever be convenient for us to serve God? Christians have turned Christ to a brand. We wear His name like a talisman. He is a guard to some, a money-doubler to another set of people, a match-maker, a visa agent, an executioner of enemies to some others. Was this why He came? We have chosen to travel the broad road of worldliness and we are preoccupied with bodily needs.

Responsible Christianity will begin when Christians realize that the kingdom of God is not of this world. The world system is a sinful system that feeds sinful nature and rewards sin, even in disguise as good works. It is impossible to reconcile the kingdom of God with the kingdom of the world, not even with good works of the most sacrificial kind. To prosper and be effective in the world, one has to bow to Satan, worship the flesh and play to the human gallery. This is the broad road to fame, wealth and power. Christians should be in the world but not be part of it; we should exist in it but not live in it; we should sojourn in it but our life must not depend on it; we should derive our daily sustenance from it but not invest our future in it. We are pilgrims passing through, ambassadors of a heavenly kingdom, servants of Christ branded in righteousness.

We are Christians because our nation needs heroes, selfless men and women who are ready to stake all and give away all. The new martyrs are individuals who submit their ambitions for others to thrive. They are people who make genuine, unknown, unacclaimed; unacknowledged sacrifices daily. That individual who welcomes a stranger; the young man who gives a helping hand to the elderly; the merciful young lady who seeks peace with an enemy; the one who turns the other cheek; the civil servant who dies a pauper rather than steal; the student who has sat for JAMB ten times rather than cheat; the policeman who is not promoted because he will not deliver bribes; the social outcast; the misfit; the conscientious lecturer who refuses to sell hand-outs - they are our heroes.

In conclusion, the church, now more than ever, must focus on doctrines, beliefs and its methods. The church is the body of Christ and His vessel for the redemption of man. The church must find ways to reform itself. One thing is sure, the church can do better by inculcating Christian responsibilities in its members and providing them with a platform for discharging these responsibilities. It must guard against reinforcing negative values. It must guard against turning Sunday mornings to dance parties - an occasion to let off steam. Fellowship should not be opportunities to escape from reality. The church should be involved in active research in order to understand the prevailing social currents and the spiritual conditions of its members so that it can prayerfully seek solutions to them. Through research, the church can remain alert, pray with purpose and act with a mission. Individual Christians should begin to reassess the value of his/her faith through the depth of his/her work in grace. A teacher must teach as Christ would. A doctor must care for his patient with compassion. In all professions and circumstances where Christians find themselves, Christ must be the standard. This standard is etched in sacrifice and packaged in love. The reason we serve is to glorify God. We live in Him and for Him. No other reason works. No ideology justifies.

"RIGHTEOUSNESS EXALTS A NATION, SIN IS A REPROACH"

Proverbs 14: 34

CHAPTER 3
Righteousness Exalts a Nation

"Righteousness exalts a nation, sin is a reproach to any people" (Prov. 14:34). Proverbs 29:2 says, "when the righteous are in authority, the people rejoice: but when the wicked beareth rule, the people mourn". "it is an abomination to kings to commit wickedness: for the throne is established by righteousness" (Prov. 16: 12). It is clear from the above that the true foundation of prosperity and the basis of stability of the throne is righteousness. No nation can make enduring progress without righteousness. Quite contrary to this fact, Nigerians are trying to achieve progress by deceit and falsehood.

One can hear Habakkuk saying:

> "Oh Lord, how long shall I cry,
> and thou wilt not save! Even
> cry out thee of violence, and
> thou wilt not save! Why dost
> thou shew me iniquity and
> cause me to behold grievance?
> For spoiling and violence are
> before me: and there are that
> raise up strife and contention.

Therefore the law is slacked, and judgement doth never go forth: for the wicked doth compass about the righteous: therefore wrong judgement proceedeth" (1: 2-4).

"Woe to me! I am as when they have gathered summer fruits, as the grape gleanings of the vintage: there is no cluster to eat: my soul desired the firstripe fruit. The good man is perished out of the earth: and there is none upright among men: they all lie in wait for blood; they hunt every man his brother in a net. That they may do evil with both handsearnestly, the prince asketh, and the judge asketh for reward; and the great man, he uttereth his mischievous desire: so they wrap it up. The best of them is as a brier: the most upright

is sharper than a thorn hedge . . .

(Micah 7: 1-4).

We characteristically deceive ourselves by referring to ours as a great nation. How foolish to think that we achieve greatness by word of mouth. We call ourselves the giant of a continent as if gigantism is worthwhile to the one who lies prostrate. This is a corrupt nation whose people are steeped in guile and very early the children are weaned on falsehood. The righteous men have perverted righteousness and the holy ones have corrupted holiness. The gods of the land take bribes; the ancestors give justice to the highest bidder. The seers do not see for nothing, the prophets cannot prophesy without inducement.

Our many prayers, fasts and conferences; our deep search into methods of praying; into the names of God; our new and improved understanding and performances of praises and adoration, our practised humility and vigorous dancing; our rehearsed tongues and choreographed prayers; our enemy bashing, binding and loosing; our prosperity tutorials, researched insights and mystical revelations have got us nowhere. We need holiness not fasting. We need to humble ourselves not cajole God. We need brokenness not excitement. We need repentance not performance. We need obedience not mysteries. God cannot be mocked.

We have become so adept at deceiving ourselves and have mistaken the oratory of men for the move of God. We ascribe the eloquence of men to the Holy Spirit. Babblings have become tongues; wishful thinking is mistaken for revelations. Mysticism is equated with faith; hunger strikes are mistaken for fasts. Greed is coated as prosperity; a good feeling is mistaken for the move of God. We keep inventing new ways to reach God as if God were deaf. We extend our fasts as if God is interested in starving us. We make a public show of it as if God has overruled himself. We invent long and noisy prayers to cover our shame. We bear offerings with defiled hands, we sing praises with false lips, and our tongues are full of the poison from wasps.

> "None calls for justice, or any
> plead for truth: they trust in
> vanity, and speak lies; they
> conceive mischief and bring
> forth iniquity".

Can fast and prayers substitute for righteousness? Can praise and adoration displace justice? Can much labour replace a pure heart before God? Is a lie true because I is said in Jesus' name? Can a thousand Hallelujahs replace repentance? Lengthy fasts are called from year to year over the same problems as if God were deaf. No one asks why. Schools are invented to teach prayers and the graduates are called warriors; yet, no war is declared against iniquity. Men groan as in labour and moan like doves and many have certificates in tongues yet they are full of profanities and vanities and have not paused to think! Fasting means nothing and prayers are useless no matter the motions, length, depth, patterns and rhythm if righteousness is lacking. The prayer of a wicked man is an abomination to God. Isaiah 58: 6-7 says "is this not the fast that I have chosen? To lose the bands of wickedness, to undo the heavy burdens on the poor; and to let to let the oppressed go free, and that ye break every yoke? Is it not to deal thy bread to the hungry and that thou bring the poor that cast out to thy house? When thou seest the naked, that thou cover him; and that thou hide not thyself from thine own flesh?" But you oppress the weak and put heavy burdens on the poor; you deny your youth a future and make orphans of children and widows of your women. When you should weep, you organise rowdy meetings to celebrate killings. Psalms 4:5 enjoins us to "offer sacrifices of righteousness and put our trust in God".

Nigeria is built on a false foundation. The pillars are held up by fraud and the roof is made of lies. The inhabitants are fed with errors and their best people are the crafty. Is this difficult to see? Politicians loot the treasury and deliver homilies of sanctity to those whose livelihood they have mortgaged. Among these are Christians who share in the 'Ghana-must-go' loot. Do we not partake in the culture of mobilization fees or the perilous 10% given upfront or underhand? In our culture, contentment has become an abomination and godliness a taboo. We revere the rich and reward them with knighthoods of various 'unsaintly' lifestyles. The crooked are the chiefs, men and women of nobility. Wickedness is rewarding and righteousness accursed.

We have murdered merit and derided hard work in the streets. Yet, we cry, pray and fast for God to judge. How will he judge when we celebrate loots with friends, relatives and spouses? Who finds something wrong when his own is the looter? We devour loots at house-warming parties, we decorate thieves with adulations at birthdays and for their gifts, we become loquacious with prayers. Whose wife has divorces her husband for his iniquity? Whose son has disowned his mother for her harlotry? Who has moved out of his father's house because he is a thief? Do we not enjoy swimming in the filth and complain only because of envy/ let everyone look to himself and to his household and hold his own accountable.

Zechariah 8: 16-17 and 7: 5-12 talk of our kind and admonishes us to "execute true judgement, and show mercy and compassion every man to his brother. And oppress not the widow, not the fatherless, the stranger, nor the poor, and let none (of us) imagine evil against his brother in (his) heart".

We are a nation that kills its young, a generation of people who live as if there is no posterity. The measure of a nation is in how it treats its weak and vulnerable. Look at the lepers crying out against us on our roads. The poor are caged; the corpses of the poor are strewn along our roads. Everyone passes by and turns away his eyes. We have made good business of misfortune. We profit from the grief of the weak. In their names, we defraud. We take the food meant for them and for evidence rub the oil on their mouths. Everyone pays lip service to development. Does development come by wishing it? We hate law and order but would not mind its benefit. We desire change, only for others but not for ourselves. Our nation is a failed project. Only repentance and God's grace can turn us around. If we persist in our present course, we will never make it as a people.

What must we do? Everyone should hold the garment of his/her brethren and let him confess his iniquity. Let every soul mourn for our wickedness. Take a day to search out your filth. Make a resolution to do well. And God will empower us to change.

"WE ARE ONLY BETTER IN THE PURSUIT OF VAINGLORY AND AVARICE.   NOTHING IS ENOUGH; WE ARE MORE KNOWLEDGEABLE BUT HAVE NO UNDERSTANDING"

Francis Egbokhare

CHAPTER 4
Entanglements

"To entangle is to get twisted up, caught up and tangled. An entanglement is a snare; something hard to get out of or get through". Have you ever seen an antelope caught in a thicket either by its horns? Or have you seen a chicken entangled in thread used for plaiting? Both situations show in a rather picturesque way how. Christians may get entangled in the affairs of the world. It is difficult to talk about entanglements without first understanding what the purpose of the Christian is. However, before we dwell on that, it is important to state that whenever we lose focus of our primary mission and our call and we begin to follow after the world's schemes, no matter how desirable, we have become entangled in a strange mission. Another way this may happen is if all the good we do, the activities we engage in, our diligent service become an end in themselves or if they become a means to our own selfish ends.

Why are we here? What is our mandate as Christians? Anything that stands in the way of the execution of our divine mandate constitutes an entanglement. Jesus said in Matthew 28:19, "Go ye therefore, and teach all nations, baptising them in the name of the Father, and the Son and the Holy Spirit".

We do not only get entangled because we are involved in fruitless dissipation or evil activities, we get entangled even in things which one would consider noble. Christians often assume that they can improve the world by being good people. It is important to be good, don't misunderstand me. There is also the dangerous belief that improvement in the living and social conditions of a people are evidence of a growing become less corrupt, at least visibly, and there is social order and economic prosperity, a people may consider themselves closer to the condition of God's will for their soul especially if they are overly religious. It is not righteousness alone that improves the social conditions of a society as we know it today. It is also a function of enlightened self-interest, skills and training, the convergence of society at some commonalities, order, conventions and rules of coexistence, exchange and behaviour. Human creativity and material potential are best expressed when there is an undisturbed linear and exponential manifestation of intellectual and physical action reinforced by belief in the value of such expression as a means to human attainment. However, this way of life is unfortunately unilinear and one-dimensional. Righteousness cuts deeper that money and the quality of life. Righteousness is not an attainment or achievement but a nature, a manner of life, an outlook of things, a condition of being, and an alternate model antagonistic to established patterns in our material existence. It is a consciousness which cannot be worked for, or attained by learning. It is awakened. We awakened into righteousness through faith in Jesus Christ, just as we are born into salvation through the Christ.

There is also a wrong belief that we commit sin, and so we strive to avoid sinning because sin is a behaviour, a breach, an attitude or a thought pattern. To some extent, this may be so if we look at its surface manifestation. However, deeper than we think is who we are. Underlying our thought and behaviour is who we are. Sin is a nature. That is why it can be inherited. We are not condemned because of what we do but because of who we are. We are sin. So, Christ was made sin in our stead. Sin is a spirit that dwells in us and overcomes our mortal bodies. This explains why our corrupt body must be crucified to let go of sin and we need a new birth to let in righteousness by the Holy Spirit. There is one sin, one sinner, one sin being. The sin is the unbelief, the sinner and the being is the devil. He has many vessels. Thus, you can understand that sin and righteousness cannot cooperate in the same being. They are two opposing seeds. This explains why there can be no improvement, reconditioning, refurbishment, transformation of the human condition. The man has to die and the world has to come to an end. The man has to die and a new being created to occupy the original divine space for the uncorrupted man. Truly speaking, a man dies when he accepts Christ and is resurrected even though the human consciousness cannot register this experience. Physical death has the benefit of material decomposition. There is a rebirth at the point where we accept Christ. Anytime a Christian is made, someone has just died and a new being reborn in his or her place. The old has truly passed away, and behold, all things have become new. The big issue then is that often we hold on to memories of the old man retained in the physical temporal form that is indwelled by the new man. Our spiritual memory in Eden persists in our instinctive hunger for God. The new nature similarly indwells our physical form but also may not be forceful in our physical consciousness. That is where the key of faith is indispensable. Faith is the key, the access code. It is a knowing and an awakening. Faith does not change a situation; it calls things that are not as though they were. Faith manifests what we are unable to see with our material sense; it is not a factor of time but of depth.

The above is a useful digression which is necessary to show us that "though we are in the world, we are not of the world". The Christian is a citizen of heaven, even though his habitation is on earth among men. If then, he begins to operate according to patterns familiar with human entities. It means that he has got himself entangled with the affairs of the world of mankind.

II Tim. 2: 3-5 states succinctly: "Thou therefore endures hardness, as a good soldier of Jesus Christ. No man that warrethentangleth himself with the affairs of this life; that he may please him who hath chosen him to be a soldier".

There is a bit of help from Colossians on how not to get entangled: chapter 3: 1-2 states:

> "If ye then be risen with Christ, seek those things which are above, where Christ sitteth on the right hand of God. Set your affection on things above, not on things on the earth".

In essence, if we set our hearts on things on earth, we are bound to get entangled with such things.

Entanglement begins with our hearts, laying up for ourselves treasures on earth and building castles in a land where we have been sent as soldiers on a rescue mission. Sitting down to wine and dine in a house where fire is raging. The primary reason we get entangled is the fact that we do not know who we are; neither do we recognise the son of whom we are. We are busy laying up for "ourselves treasures upon earth, where moth and rust doth corrupt and where thieves break in" (Matt. 6:20). It is clear according to verse 20 of the same chapter that where our treasures are, there will our hearts also be. Basically, we spend our time doing things that are of value to us and we focus on the treasures of life.

Romans 12:2 admonishes us not to be conformed to this world. To conform is "to act according to law and rule; be in agreement with generally accepted standards of business, law, conduct, or worship". It does look confusing at first considering the fact that it is important for us to obey laws and authorities. However, the term 'world' stands for a pattern, a scheme of things, a dispensation, a flow, and a consciousness that rules our present age. II Tim. 3:1-5 makes a list of some patterns of the world. It states:

"This know also, that in the last days perilous times shall come. For men shall be lovers of their own selves, covetous, boasters, proud, blasphemers, disobedient to parents, unthankful, unholy. Without natural affection, trucebreakers, false accusers, incontinent, fierce, despisers of those that are good, traitors, heady, high-minded, lovers of pleasures more than God, having a form of godliness, but denying the power thereof, from such turn away".

Galatians 5: 19 gives us more insight into the patterns of the world: "Now the works of the flesh are manifest which are these: adultery, fornication, uncleanness, lasciviousness, idolatry, witchcraft, hatred, variance, emulations, wrath, strife, seditions, heresies, envying and such like . . ."

The world as often used in the bible refers to the flesh. The patterns of the world refer to those attributes that are established human propensities, the things that men hold dear and cherish, and the practices that drive our commerce and value system. It is effortless to identify certain practices as sin and avoid them. What is more difficult to do is to see evil in some other practices that have been established as values but which are indeed booby traps that deceive the undiscerning. The subtle features are the dangerous entanglements.

Let us look at the pattern of fashion to which most of us are sold. The basic ideology of fashion, especially amongst women, is to flaunt what should be hidden. What are not standard moderate fashions were unpardonable decades ago. No one quarrels about off-shoulder clothes today slits are getting longer, skirts are getting shorter. Everything now bulges no matter from which angle one looks. It is most difficult to tell that a person is a Christian by his or her attire. We are as loud and tempting as any other person in the street. I can understand that every lady wants to be attractive and that people would want to enhance their looks by using all kinds of accessories, attachments and make over. The question is what is the spirit behind it? In spite of the fact that people, generally want to look more "attractive", more ladies are not getting married and men are not anymore faithful to their wives. Marriages are worse now than they once were. Something is surely desperately wrong. It is so difficult to put a form to godliness or to ascribe certain lifestyles to Christians. How can one tell a Christian lady from a common street woman? How does one distinguish between a Christian man and a roadside hemp-smoking hippy? There appears also to be no form to manliness. When we see youths today with hoops around their ears and "dreadlocks", one can relate to their folly. Yes, on the streets, why not? However, in the church, there must be some balance.

A commercial spirit has overtaken our generation. From the home to the church, people are buying and selling and transacting businesses. Shops have been set up in the souls of men and their consciousness is a busy marketplace. We are now so entangled with mammon to the point that we trade in spiritual gifts. We buy and sell prayers and invent strategies for legitimising greed. Church leaders have perfected self-advertisement and sales promotion.

The name of Jesus is used as bait to lure people to trade fairs called crusades. There are so many terms in the world that give a good expression to human greed. Greed is couched as aggressive investment, manipulation is described as advertisement, cunning is sales promotion and deceit is called marketing. The same standards used by the world are also used by Christians; the laws of man apply also in the church. Where are Christians' principles in the Nigerian finance sector where usury predominates? The credit system is a value of modern finance systems. It has become so accepted that one will not be surprised if churches are into the business of lending our money. We are all now trapped by the beast of a financial system. Our convenience more than anything prevents us from looking closely at the pattern of things. We are all faithfully involved in the stock exchange and we participate in all kinds of gambling called gaming shows. Lottery is no longer questioned. No one raised his or her voice against any financial practice as long as profit is raked in. Every conversation ends with money. Soon, we will be bearing the mark of the beast. In spite of increased income and greater skills at making money, families are still not more harmonious. Everyone wants more and the more we have, the more we desire. What has happened to good old contentment?

Let me not query here the world economic order and the principles underlying the financial system. One can only say that these are based on human imperfections and propensities notwithstanding the principles that justify them. I think we should not work to sustain an order that puts a price on human life.

Advertising plays on man's greed. In the present world, manufacturers and businesses create needs and not products as people are often made to believe. People are bombarded with manipulative advertisements that create in them appetites that will never be satisfied. They are given products that have inbuilt obsolescence. If a consumer good does not have addictive substances, advertisement ensures that people are hooked. If parents cannot be reached, children are used as tools to get into their pockets. We are now like genetically engineered pigs, fed with vitamins and hormones, fattened for the slaughter. Consumerism is a condition of modern man. Accumulation has turned most people to collectors of antiques. There is a growing acceptance of a lifestyle that has turned many homes to junkyards.

One virus that afflicts or world is 'busy-ness'. To be busy and to be able to handle multiple assignments (multi-tasking) is a sign of success and sophistication. What are we busy doing? Being so busy doesn't necessarily mean that we are doing more than our ancestors did. We have only just lost the art of quiet meditation and healthy relaxation. We are only better in the pursuit of vainglory and avarice. Nothing is enough; we are more knowledgeable but have no understanding. We have better sight but lack perception. The world is now so noisy with hypnotism. People have no time to think. Some think they are suffering because someone has suggested it to them. Many think they are victims and fail to take responsibility. Christians need to break free, stop for a while, shut their eyes, listen within and they will feel the truth about the world.

One other area of entanglement is our concept and pursuit of leisure. Leisure is driven by an unhealthy desire for passion and pleasures. The television serves this in doses of pornography, soap opera, reality shows and all the night drama primed to promote a delusion and a lifestyle. We are made to believe that pleasure brings happiness, and that life is about indulging ourselves. The promotion of vices and harmless pastimes is one of the deceits of modern lifestyles. How are Christians faring with leisure? Families who can ill-afford it undertake expensive vacations; the outcomes do not bring relaxation but tension and deceit. The entertainment industry is full of all kinds of miscreants who are packaged and positioned as role models. Our youths are made to believe that they represent the best in human attributes. Hero worship is the modern form of idolatry. Church music differs only in lyrics. However, by and large the rhythm tells the story very well performed in the world. In the church, the hero is not the man in the street but his mirror image pastor-man whose mannerisms are a perfect copy of the street lad.

It is time to disentangle ourselves from the myriad of unnecessary activities and focus on pleasing God everyday of our lives.

"FEAR CAN KEEP US UP ALL NIGHT LONG BUT FAITH MAKES ONE FINE PILLOW"

PHILLIP GULLEY

CHAPTER 5
Doubt (Matthew 14)

Peter focused on Jesus and so was able to walk on water. He was looking at Jesus, not the water. Thus, he did what Jesus did. Peter listened to Jesus; so, he heard His call and moved to Him. He did not listen to the wind, the storm and the restless sea. He could hear the voice of Jesus loud and clear saying "COME".

When he lost his focus, he could see the turbulence of the watery deep and his mind overwhelmed by the depths and its destruction; he began to sink into that which he feared. When he looked to see; it was the fierce storm that he beheld and could hear the mighty thunder of the waters. He could hear Jesus no more saying "Be of good cheer; it is I: be not afraid". His feet were as pillars of fear at the sight of the troubled waters; he could not hear Christ saying: "COME". Faith is active, on the move. It never stops in its tracks. Doubt is a weight that puts a clog in one's heart.

In faith we move forward to Christ. In doubt, we sink down with troubles. Whose voice do we hear, our Lord or our troubles? Whose counsel do we trust, our God or our circumstances? Whether we move or stop, who we see or what we see all determine where we stand in faith or doubt.

Faith means that we keep moving. Thus, the problem of the unprofitable servant was not only that he did not make profit, but that he did not exercise faith. There was no dynamic force in his service. When we invest our talents, we are active in faith. Faith cannot stop just as it is a natural law that an object in motion in the air, falls to the ground once it stops moving. Faith becomes dead when inactive (see James 2: 14-26).

So what should we do?

In any situation, find out what Christ is saying. Move in the direction of His word. Do not trust in your circumstances, trust in God. That is faith. Doubt is not trusting God enough.

It is important to note that the wind was still there when Peter obeyed Christ's voice but his attention was on Christ. Thus, his doubt or trust was not a function of the circumstances, but of Peter's shift of focus. Jesus calmed the storm. Our faith calms our storms if we hold on long enough.

"GLUTTONY KILLS MORE THAN THE SWORD AND IS THE FOREMENTER OF ALL EVILS"

Fr. Patricius

CHAPTER 6
Attitude to Food

The significance of Daniel's position is much lost because the focus is often on the fact that Daniel was God-fearing. However, the fact that he refused to eat meat and good food was not just because the food was associated with some religious practices (we are not told so), but for the reason that Daniel must have had enough spiritual consciousness to realise that he had to liberate himself from the control of human appetites. Significantly, Christ was to demonstrate the need for this, years later.

1. He overcame the temptation of the devil and reaffirmed God's word to the Israelites that man must not live by bread alone, but by every word that proceeds out of the mouth of God.

2. Christ tells us that He is the bread of life that endures onto eternal life. A food-dominated person cannot be spiritual. This is why gluttony is a sin. You are food-dominated to the extent that you are unable to appreciate the role of food as sustenance and not as a life giving source.

Daniel demonstrated that the word is not nutritious only in a spiritual sense but also in a physical one – as it turned out he looked better than those who were feeding sumptuously.

In the process of striving for spiritual growth, we cannot also grow appetites. We cannot grow in fleshly terms and grow in spiritual terms at the same time. We cannot derive more of the world and more of heaven at the same time. We cannot worship God and mammon at the same time. Christ's caution bout anxiety over food, clothing and other issues in Matthew 6 is not only because of the folly of worrying, but to tell us that if we worry about the kingdom of God and about righteousness, God will meet other needs. We are counselled not to run after worldly things, possessions, food, drinks, clothes and money. We cannot run after God's kingdom and earthly comfort at the same time. If we treasure these things, we cannot as a matter of truth, also treasure righteousness and God's kingdom.

Our first duty in life should be to treasure the kingdom of God. We must be liberated from the pursuit of human security. We need to guard against spiritual chains. Furthermore, we need to focus on attaining spiritual liberty because human liberty follows as a natural consequence.

Remember, it is important to attain inner peace rather than just calming external chaos.

"HYPOCRISY IS FOLLY"

Cecil

CHAPTER 7
Silence as a Spiritual Exercise

The words we speak are a reflection of our state of mind and our thoughts. "Out of the abundance of the heart, the mouth speaketh". Thoughts are expressed either in words or actions. So words are actions expressed in a verbal form. Actions are words of physical kind. God judges us on the basis of our intentions or motives. At a deeper level, intentions determine the value of what we say or do words are important, not only by the fact that they reveal our thought's state and consequently the purity of our hearts, but they form one firm basis upon which judgement will be made.

Matt. 12: 36-37 says ". . . every idle word that men shall speak, they shall give account thereof in the Day of Judgement. For by thy words, thou shall be judged and by thy words thou shall be condemned".

If words will play such an important role in how we are judged, we ought to speak circumspectly not carelessly. If we must speak at all, we ought not to speak if we will speak ill. The bible contains so much which we can condense into a set of principles on how to speak.

Matt. 7:1 says "Judge not that ye be not judged. For with what judgement ye judge, ye shall be judged". And with what measure ye make, it shall be measured to you again. This is explained in verses 3, 4 and 5.

This should be understood to mean that we should tolerate evil conduct or keep quiet when things are going wrong. This is a caution against condemnation and running down people for this is essentially founded on evil intentions, self-righteousness and self-justification. The case of how Jesus handled the adulterous woman drives home the point that we are all guilty. It shows also that judgement of condemnation comes out of hypocrisy. Jesus shows us the right judgement to make – a correction founded on love, compassion, and pity.

The story of the praying Pharisee and the Publican also clearly shows how a judging and hypocritical heart functions. It is all a matter of self-justification and using oneself as a measuring standard. We stand condemned when we do this because we leave our own spiritual needs unattended to. We become spiritual *agbero*. The right spirit is demonstrated by the Publican. We are all spiritual publicans, because we cannot of our own attain righteousness- it is grace that makes us right with God. Our righteousness in itself falls far short of God's standard even at its best. So, a truly spiritual person is in recognition of his own state and so concentrates on making spiritual progress not on pummelling another person or condemning others. He ends up being spiritually justified before God. Hypocrisy is not just a character trait; it is also a spiritual one. It is a form of spiritual blindness.

The tragic thing about hypocrisy is that one thinks he/she has attained spirituality. He becomes so critical and uncompassionate, not out of love for God but from a haughtiness of spirit, a spiritual pride. In this state, God becomes irrelevant in a true sense as the man places himself at par with the all-righteous God. The fact that He judges is in fact a usurpation of God's right and authority as the true and righteous judge of all creation.

So, next time you think about hypocrites, do not limit your understanding only to the physical and legalistic sense of those who do not keep the law even though they would like us to think that they do. Think of the spiritual diversion of those who are blind spiritually in the sense that they do not have any knowledge of their spiritual helplessness. It is important for us to practice silence. Silence enables us to scale our thoughts for words. Always remember that you could be wrong and your passion will be measured.

Do you realize that there is a chance that you are wrong about that strong and holy position you hold, about that person? If you do, you will measure your zeal with caution and your judgement with consideration. Remember that you are human and vulnerable and the haste to condemn will diminish; remember that your talents were given not invented and your impatience with inferiors will be replaced by understanding. Your best deeds will one day be forgotten and you will be replaced by understanding. Your best deeds will one day be forgotten and you will be humbled in your conceit.

"DO NOT DESPISE THE DAYS OF LITTLE BEGINNINGS"

CHAPTER 8
The Dignity of Labour and the God of Work

The bible shows clearly that God is a God of work. If we are truly created in the image of God, we must work.

"And on the seventh day God ended his work which he had made: and he rested on the seventh day from all his work which he had made".

Genesis 2:2

"My father worketh hitherto and I work".

John 5:17

"Neither give place to the devil. Let him that stole steal no more: but rather let him labour, working with his hand the thing which is good, that he may have to give him that needeth".

Ephesians 4:27-28

"And that ye study to be quiet, and to do your own business, and to work with your own hands, as we commanded you. That ye may walk honestly toward them that are without, and that ye may have lack of nothing".

I Thessalonians 4:11-12

". . .For even when we were with you, this we commanded you, that if any would not work, neither should he eat".

II Thessalonians 3:8-10

What does Dignity of Labour Mean?

There is no such thing as a job that is beneath one's status as long as one makes an honest living. We must learn to enjoy the work of our hands and be proud to be productively engaged. Every work we do is important to the extent that we earn our living through it and render a service to other people. We must be proud of our work and learn to take pleasure in it instead of lamenting and being ashamed.

Some people have nothing because they are too ashamed to be involved in certain professions while some focus on what others are doing because they believe such jobs are more dignifying.

Others are greedy, they cannot bear to earn a little, and they spend the whole of their life waiting for the big job and so become unemployable. No one wants to engage a person without a record of employment.

Still others are lazy. They are not willing to pay the price of hard work. Laziness explains why people often go from church to church seeking that magical message that will give them the dream job.

The Problem of Mindset and Fixations

My pastor does not want to help. Who is helping your pastor?

- My relatives are wicked that is why I am suffering. I have no helper. Who are you helping? Take your future in your own hands.
- The government is not creating jobs. Why don't you create one if no one cares about you?
- I have no money to start a business. So what have you to start with? Suppose I find you money here and now, what are you going to do with it?

It is tragic when people develop a poverty mentality or when they seek to be pitied by people with lesser endowments. It is most painful to see able bodied people develop a beggar complex where more and more physically challenged people are seeking their own independence.

- A pressing need is for people to change their habits of thinking. Remember, as a man thinketh in his heart so is he.
- Cultivate hope instead of helplessness.
- Embrace faith instead of despairing.
- Look to yourself instead of blaming others.
- Take action instead of grumbling.

For example, people are looking for trustworthy and humane individuals who will assist them in providing care to aged parents and children, cleaning services, clearing of lawns and supervision of projects. One of the biggest headaches today in our land is the preponderance of fake products and fake people. Remember, honesty is a sellable trait.

Getting Started

Life is about choices. Our failure or success in life is a function of the accumulation of the positive or negative choices we have made. A person who has nothing doing is a sluggard. Do something even if you are not in paid employment. You could volunteer and help out. God meets people in the context of their work (Gideon, Peter). Start with the things you know how to do well or that you enjoy doing.

Francis Egbokhare

Cultivate service. Work because you want to meet a need not because you want to mine money. Search for a need and try to meet it. One critical area of need today is care provision. People are looking for honest and diligent workers; not intelligent crooks. Pay attention to the little pennies – do not despise the days of little beginnings. Therefore, launch out into the deep and let down your nets for a bountiful harvest.

CHAPTER 9
Life

Do you ever wonder what this life is all about? The meaning of everything? Some people have asked, if there is God, why does He allow pain and death? Is it really God that allows pains and death? When we lose people close to us, we are filled with confusion. We may even ask why? Death is painful not because of the dead but the living. It is merely a reminder of our mortality, the futility of our accumulation and vanity of our ambitions. More than death, it is perhaps fear that is the greatest enemy of mankind. Many of us are in captivity. We fear everything. We are afraid of people and afraid of the future. Fear becomes one big weight that limits our potentials and confines us to misery. Life is like the Universe.

The universe is made of materials of various densities. Humans live on different planes in the visible world just as different creatures in the sea thrive at different depths. We live in one planet but thrive in diverse worlds. We are dense matter of diverse spiritual cohesion. Our denseness is a function of the spiritual order that rule our lives. On a horizontal level, we are all subject to the same forces that act on our material form. At a dimensional level, we live in multi-universe within the planet called earth. There are

71

forces that drag us down the depths or pulls us up the heights. Our consciousness is the grid to which these forces connect, a kind of umbilical.

Law, sin, heaven, hell, good, evil, etc. are human terms improperly conceptualised by human language just as time is a function of human perception. How does one eliminate time as a concept or modify its reality when human perception can capture only two points in an endless continuum – i.e. the emergence of matter into visible realm and its extinguision from the same realm.

Part of the dilemma of mankind is not only the conceptualisation of infinity of the different states matter vis-à-vis human sensory capabilities but also the boundedness of matter, event, space, etc. we place boundaries and isolate events; we deal with reality by drawing lines and parsing up experience. We identify individuals and see life as isochronous with persons not communities. We think in a past, present and future continuum not in a timeless orbit and circle of renewal. One of the problems of mankind comes from the illusion of the person, the lines and points we have identified, the focus on the part and our inability to focus on the whole.

There are no good words to capture the values of our oneness, no vocabulary to emphasise our collectivity. Our languages are deficient in expressing the high order of the human brotherhood and so we cannot think without much effort about our common good. Thus, it is natural for us to see ourselves primarily in terms of our opposition to others. We define our reality against that of others; calculate our progress in competition against others, use others as a ground against which we pitch ourselves as figures. If we know that we are one, we will stop to compete but cooperate instead. Wars will cease because we will understand that territoriality is a concept of a debased consciousness. Nationalism will be recognised in its true form as sin. We will stop trade and promote exchange and sharing. It is an unbelievable tragedy, how we have organised ourselves into groups to exploit one another and negotiate advantages at the expense of the majority. How we have shared up our common resources for group and individual advantage. The material conception and violence and accumulation. In our experience, we are motivated by a grand desire for personal success, which in fact, is no success at all. Whenever the advantage of the one leads to disadvantage of the other, or where the progress of a few leads to the disadvantage of the majority, success cannot be imputed to the bargain, no matter what intellectual or ideological framework supports the argument. Sin is a general condition of human spiritual poverty. It is not just a function of an individual's behaviours; it is the structures and system that limits the achievements of higher consciousness by the human soul. The human purpose at the moment is guided by a corrupted consciousness. Even the best acts of courage and works of charity cannot measure up to the standards of a system where the individual serves the human race and where he or she is an expression of its many virtues. As I look at the way we make wars, and listen to the great arguments that support our ideas, I see a people who are primed to self-destruct. From the Middle East where brothers are locked in ancient animosities and circles of revenge and bitterness, to the many so-called struggles for self-determination, I see delusions. We cannot achieve our greatness by destroying part of us. Liberty cannot come through domination, just as it is an illusion to attain freedom through bloodshed. Until we recognise that we are part of one another, that defining human achievement at the common mundane level of beastly struggles is our primary limitation, we remain exposed to the extermination of our species.

F rancis Egbokhare is a teacher in the Department of Linguistics and African Languages, University of Ibadan, Nigeria. He speaks regularly in churches on the need to cultivate integrity in Christian life. He has published a book of Christian poems and has several tracts written and circulated under the label Ezra Project and Integrity Incorporated.

Brother Francis believes that change will come when truly committed Christians live as witnesses in their places of work and communities. He believes that the professional work of Christians matters as much to God as their Christian worship.

Francis Egbokhare

www.ingramcontent.com/pod-product-compliance
Lightning Source LLC
Chambersburg PA
CBHW060350050426
42449CB00011B/2909